GEORGIA PETERKIN

WHAT I TELL MYSELF

DAILY EMOTIONAL, MENTAL & SPIRITUAL MOTIVATIONS AND MANTRAS

VOL II

WHAT I TELL MYSELF

ISBN: 979-8-89283-084-3

Cover Design:

Interior Formatting: Nonon Tech & Design

Available on Amazon.

This book is presented to

_____

On this date:

_____

ACKNOWLEDGMENTS

I met Angelique Romou in 2016 when I hosted the "Lady of Excellence Gala" which attracted more than one hundred and fifty women in attendance. She was recommended to me when I was looking for an MC. When we spoke about what I was doing, she was more excited than I was! That was a win for me. From then onwards, she was with me all through the steps and preparations, till the day of the event. She was generous with her advice, her assistance—she was "all hands on deck".

On the day of the event, we (Angelique and I) went to the venue to oversee the setup. When we went in, she looked around, looked at me with eyes wide open, and said, "What is this?" Without waiting for my response, she continued, "These dinner wares must change, these napkins must go." I said, "Angelique, I am spent out! There's no more budget." She said, "I am sorry; this event is called 'Lady of Excellence' of which I am a part. Therefore, the venue and everything must be nothing short of excellence; let's go!"

We got into her jeep and went shopping for what was obviously more appropriate for the setting. We drove around and she didn't hesitate or hold back on spending. She didn't give it a second thought but was all in with her heart as though it was her very own event. This, for me, is what true sisterhood and women's empowerment is all about. I guess I can say Angelique covered my nakedness so no one would see it. And if I didn't talk about it, no one would know.

Thereafter, I observed her; I have known her to be unselfish, and supportive. Having me on her TV program (A Better Place), and inviting me on her radio program, which by the way, is also another aspect of her love for humanity and youths. Angelique is simply a phenomenal lady. We've had moments of girls' time and all I ever felt from her is pure love and sincerity.

She inspires me with her actions both in her governmental roles and as an individual.

Thank you, Angelique J.G. Romou *(Member of Parliament)*.

FOREWORD

Some years ago, a very dynamic lady who was embarking on a journey of excellence approached me.

The topic Georgia was

asking me to assist her with was ETIQUETTE, which was dear to my heart. So, once I was asked, I immediately said 'yes'. Together, we embarked on this journey many years ago and have remained friends ever since. Not one day would go by without Georgia sending a word of encouragement or scripture of inspiration to me. Georgia is unwavering in her dedication to the word called, "positivity," and finds every way possible to share positive words with everyone she encounters. I was given the opportunity to have a sneak peek at this work of art and immediately felt compelled to give it my seal of approval. Being a motivational speaker myself, it gives me the honor to say, "Job well done, Georgia!" I know this book will inspire and encourage many. I do hope that this is just the beginning of many more excellent works to come.

Congratulations, my sister, may the good Lord continue to uplift you and give you the strength to continue writing and inspiring others, as my motto is, "I am living and having an attitude of gratitude." I am grateful for you. Continue to soar, my sister!

—MP Angelique J.G. Romou

AUTHOR'S NOTE

We often hear the phrase, "No man is an island," which is true. We all need and rely on others for one thing or the other. Life, from its foundation, was intended for human beings to be interdependent. However, over the years, we have seen a decline in interdependency, as people become more self-absorbed, or simply find themselves in a survival mode. This could be through circumstances such as: intentional abandonment, the loss of loved ones, the business of life, and the challenges of not being able to balance work-family, friendships. This can leave you feeling empty, alone, unloved, unappreciated, and rejected.

In times like these, it is important for you to find inner strength and acknowledge that everyone is dealing with their own issues (some are more or less challenging than what you are currently facing). I often revert to a verse in the Bible that says:

Now David was greatly distressed, for the people spoke of stoning him because the soul of all the people was grieved, every man for his sons and his daughters. But David strengthened himself in the LORD his God. — I Sam 30:6

Though David had a crowd around him, he felt alone and afraid because everyone was now looking out for themselves and that included even thinking about hurting King David because they thought he was the cause of their problems. He had to gather every ounce of strength within him to "ENCOURAGE HIMSELF." Life, today, is no different! We must learn to encourage ourselves.

Someone once said, "When the going gets tough, the tough gets going." For those of us who know the word of God, we can rely on the pages of the Bible to give us comfort and hope. Other times, through our experiences, we birth words, phrases, quotes, and mantras that help us cope and give us a new perspective to life.

This book helps you with that. As you scroll through the pages, my hope is that you find at least one quote that will give you that extra boost to push, hope, live, and accept the world as it comes and accept people as they are.

These quotes are to encourage you to be strong, to see life and people through a different lens–one that is more tolerant, accepting, responsible, strong, and loving who you are a little more.

I have come to realize that many quotes in this era are breeding narcissism. I want to make this clear that I am totally for interdependency! I believe and encourage partnership, and supporting each other, even while we maintain healthy boundaries and respect for each other. We must never believe that we are so independent and strong that we don't need anyone; this could not be farther from the truth.

Happy reading!

WHAT I TELL MYSELF

DAILY EMOTIONAL, MENTAL & SPIRITUAL MOTIVATIONS, AND MANTRAS

WHAT I TELL MYSELF

1.   I am grateful that I am still here despite it all.

I am grateful that I have an attitude of gratitude.

I am grateful for the friends I have, even if they're not a lot.

I am grateful that I can pay at least one of my bills.

I don't have a lot, but I am grateful for what I have.

I am grateful that I still have strength that allows me to work.

I am grateful that I have ideas that can be turned into successful reality.

I am grateful for this moment.

2. You are stronger than you think. Your bad days often prove that. Appreciate those bad days, they build character and provoke, at least, two of the fruits of the spirit—Patience and self-control.

3. God's decision is my choice, God's choice is what I choose. I have made enough mess making choices on my own, and I have seen enough success from choices chosen by God.

4. God has always been the only hope. Human beings made Him the last hope, because we try everything before we try God.

5. God is not careless about His promises. He pays attention to what He promises and makes sure to fulfil them accordingly.

6. The righteous calls and God answers, the wicked shout but God doesn't hear.

7. The only person I follow blindly is the omniscient all-seeing God of heaven and earth. Others must show me where we are headed... I need to see.

8. Fear can cause you to make impetuous and costly decisions. Have nothing to do with fear. It is one of, if not the biggest enemies to your progress, moving on or letting go.

9. I have no pride when it comes to worshipping God, but I take pride in what I do for His Kingdom.

10. Allow yourself to be distracted occasionally. It can be the break that you really need and return to focus with a new perspective that serves you well.

11. It is okay, you are doing your best, even if the results are not evident yet. Keep doing and have faith in yourself and in God's timing.

12. I have trusted so many wrong people throughout my life and all it got me was pain, hurt and deception. Now, I trust you, Lord, with all my life for the rest of my life.

13. Ask yourself, "How are you feeling today?" Then respond...

Ask again: "Would you like to talk about how you are feeling?" Then respond...

If you would like to talk about it, find one person you know for certain who will listen and talk to them.

And if you can't, then look at yourself in the mirror and tell yourself something encouraging and give yourself a compliment.

14. When the game ends, the camera and media do not follow the losing team to the Locker Room. Sometimes in life, only when everything is all over do we see the real winner, the real people, and the real facts.

15. Love means nothing if not shared; happiness is useless if it cannot be expressed. Your achievements are lonely with no one to celebrate with. Why cry when the reason is unknown? Your smile is a waste without a reflection or appreciation. The answer to all of this is, we all need each other to express our emotions and achievements. Life will be lonely with only yourself to share with.

16. Be encouraged. Failing does not make you a failure. But it sure does show that you are TRYING. Keep on trying; you will get it right one day. (#thebenefitofpersistency)

17. There's a type of woman who knows her role in the relationship and doesn't have to prove anything because she validates herself and her husband approves of her totally. She knows how much her husband loves and respects her, so she never feels threatened by other females around him. Her husband includes her in everything and is proud to have her by his side wherever he goes. She knows exactly what he will say or do in any situation, so she is never surprised by his action but always surprised by the things he does to please her. Is this story about HER? Or maybe about a GOOD MAN?

18. A simple or small act of kindness can create a lasting ripple effect.

19. Stand tall in faith but be humble in your success. Choose your circle wisely, but never reject or treat others like outcasts.

20. There is the "promise" and the "permitted." God will permit some things for various reasons, more commonly because of our impatience, our inability to heed God's voice and directions, and our desire to make right what went wrong (TAKING MATTERS IN OUR OWN HANDS–TRYING TO HELP GOD). But the permitted can never take the place of promise. The permitted can look good, feel good, be around for a very long time, and produce many wonderful things that we confuse for the "PROMISE." Good things can come out of the permitted by God's mercy. But great fulfilling things–the best things–will come out of the "PROMISE." Have the faith and flexibility to disconnect from the permitted so you can join and connect to the "PROMISE."

21. David was unafraid to contend with bad-mouthing Goliath who defied the God of Israel. Likewise, we should not be afraid to contend with those who defy our faith and the LORD our GOD, knowing that God will fight against those who fight against us.

22. God cannot be fathomed, but He certainly can be trusted.

23. Who are we really? Why do we live unconscionable lives without regard or remorse for the people around us? Who we hurt, who we use, who we disrespect, who we look down on, who we steal from, who we refuse to help, as though we are invincible, we are mighty in our own eyes. We live in this vast obscurity as though there is no end to us and our doings. We act as though there is none greater, better, or more powerful than us. If only we could see ourselves through the eyes of the Creator who formed us from DUST out of love, mercy, grace, and compassion.

24. Comfort your heart; speak peace to your soul. Let God be magnified. He delivers the righteous from the hands of the wicked and evil man.

25. Satisfy her emotions, and she will never commit to another; give her attention, and her eyes will always be on you and never any other.

26. Never miss the opportunity to do the will of God. It is what others see in you and us as a compass that leads to faith.

27. Keep your eyes open and always look around. But only to pay attention to the good in others and see the pitfall and temptation that your adversaries have set up against you.

28. Queens do not flaunt sexiness; they promulgate elegance. Likewise, kings do not parade macho; they exercise authority, integrity, and command.

29. A strong man is known for his ability to control himself and rule his emotions. A real man is known for his integrity and honor.

30. If it is for sale, then it is not love. I am neither a buyer nor a seller of love. Love comes freely and should be given and received freely.

31. Be excited about meeting the newer version of you that is coming slowly but surely. As you meet him or her, be enthusiastic about presenting the new you to the world. You have gone through the test of time, survived, and are ready to live freely, strongly, and boldly.

32. There are people in the world that can benefit a great deal from your love and compassion. Just notice them around you and give as you go.

33. There should be a purpose in each of our hearts, not to partake in the ungodly or defiled thing even if we have trouble following through on what we have purposed. It should unwaveringly be the desire of our hearts; only by this will God find us faithful, righteous, and worthy to be called, "man or woman after my heart."

34. None of us is an afterthought in the mind of God. He thought of us long before we came into existence. He fashioned us in his mind before he formed us. He knew all our life stories before we lived them, and He made provision and preparation for every single line in our story, be it good or bad. *You are important, she is important, he is important, they are important, we are important to God.

35. God is love; He loves you. Just love yourself enough to believe that you are worthy of His love.

36. The goodness of God and the love of God allow Him to hear you from wherever you are and listen

to whoever and whatever you are. Speak to Him in your own unique way, the best way you know how to.

37.   It does not matter how hard it gets, how impossible things may seem, I will be comfortable, complete, satisfied, and victorious in the end. How it ends is what matters. The end will decide what I am made of.

38.   Set your standard high and be comfortable doing so without permission. Those who are meant to permanently be a part of your journey will not have a problem with your set standard.

39.   As long as you do not lose yourself in the process, it is okay to lose something or someone.

40.   Some will find fault and criticize what they cannot control or understand. It is easier for them than to accept your idiosyncrasies.

41.   Do not let your romantic sentiments override your better judgment.

42. Trust in God and believe that whatever He does is well done, and whatever He makes is perfectly made, including "YOU." You are a work of art done by the Master of Art—Jehovah God.

43. Do not boast about yourself, what you are, who you are, or what you've achieved. But boast in the knowledge of knowing God chose you.

44. Perfectly imperfect, flawlessly flawed, humbly proud to be me. I was carefully made to be ME–every little detail–the way I walk, talk, look, smile, and frown. All of it was designed to make me who I am.

45. You are not a mistake; you are a choice God chose. Accept and celebrate your existence.

46. If you were to answer or react to everything in life because you are right, you would end up being the loser in the game that was set for you to win.

47. Do not ask permission to achieve or succeed. Great advice is important, not permission.

48. As individuals, we do not have the power to choose what others say to us or their choice of words. But we have the power to decide what and who we respond or react to. Understand that not everything or everyone is worth your time or attention.

49. I will no longer compromise my standard; I will stand hard. My integrity is non-negotiable, neither is it for sale.

50. Passionately envision yourself where you want to be and with whom you want to be. It sets the stage for you to run and work towards your vision.

51. Dreams are free; everybody can afford to dream. Achieving what you dream is expensive. Not everyone wants to pay the price, and not everyone can afford the price.

52. Do not get tired of hearing yourself repeating your dreams and aspirations.

53. If you don't know where you want to be or where you are going, you will start on a journey and end up nowhere.

54. I am the perfect picture of nothing, yet the perfect example of everything great.

55. Value yourself and show up. Do not praise yourself and show off. Be proud to have been chosen, but do not choose to be proud.

56. You love someone the way they want to be loved, not how you want to love them. Remember your way of loving, as good as it may seem, might not be appealing or desirous to the receiver.

57. Don't forget to take good care of yourself, including forgiving yourself even before you forgive others. #selflove #selfacceptance #selfappreciation #selfcare# #selfrespect

58. Dare to do that which has never been done, seen or heard before. Be different, be creative, and be unique. And be ready for the critiques of your creativity.

59. When God ordains love, it cannot be broken by problems, weakened over time, or destroyed by distance. True love has true power and longevity to endure all things.

60. God uses difficult people as sandpaper to rub off all our rough edges that come in the form of impatience, anger, unforgiveness, hate, and selfishness. These people are used to developing good character in us.

61. It is much better to acknowledge when and where we went wrong and say, "I am sorry." Too often, we allow pride and ego to rob us of a beautiful friendship, relationship, marriage, or position.

62. Proverbs 16:2-3: "All the ways of a man are good in his own eyes, but the LORD weighs the spirit. Commit your ways unto the LORD, and your thoughts shall be established." Verse 9: "A man's heart plans his way, but the LORD directs all his steps."

We should be humble enough to know and accept that we are mortals, and as such, we are prone to mistakes and misjudgment. On the other hand, God who is immortal, knows what was, what is, and what will be. We often suffer losses, hurt, and pain because we do not wait and seek direction from God. There are times our plans fail, not because they were not great plans but because we think of ourselves as self-sufficient. We get carried away by our strength and wisdom, and we forget about the omnipotent, omnipresent, omniscient One, that it is He who directs all our ways. If we bring our plans and desires to Him, He will direct our steps, establish our ways and bring our plans to pass.

63. "WE" is greater than "I," "US" is stronger than "ME," and "OUR" is more powerful than "MY." We are good alone but so much better together.

64. Be careful of sympathizing with hypocrites and private enemies. They are usually very close to you and seemingly nice to you.

65. Remember the "SOMETIMES of LIFE." Sometimes, our spirit gets crushed to save our soul. Sometimes, our hearts are broken to make us whole. Sometimes, we feel pain so that we can be stronger. Sometimes, we experience illness so that we can take better care of our health. Sometimes, we lose everything so we can appreciate what is given.

66. I have never seen an advertisement for Rolls Royce, Bentley, Austin Martin, or Bugatti. The reason for this is simple–they know their products bring "worthy customers" to them. LESSON: When you know your value, you do not advertise for relationship of any kind, position or recognition. You do not beg people to like you or spend time with or invest in you. Be confident in yourself as a product made by God without any factory defect. Not everyone can afford the luxury of your presence or friendship, only those who knows your value.

67. Husbands, cherish your wife privately, praise her publicly. Show her off like a grand prize to onlookers. Let her not only feel but know that out of all the millions of women in the world, she is the one you choose, love, and need.

68. It's not my walk; it's not my talk; it's not my beauty; it's not my social status; it's not even my worship. It's nothing about me but everything about God. It's how He fashioned, cared for, filled me, and let His grace flow over me, keeping me all the way, in every way.

69. Wife, honor your husband and serve him as the only man that matters to you. Treat him as a king in the home, and respect and acknowledge him publicly. Appreciate all his efforts, support him in all he does, and celebrate his achievements like he is your hero. Let your home be peaceful, clean, and welcoming for him. Let your husband lead you; don't deprive him of his God-given role.

> Everyone looks **OKAY** is doing **OKAY** until you have a **DEEP CONVERSATION** with them.

@GeorgiaPeterkin

70. Being confident does not mean you are proud. Being proud is thinking you are above everyone else or better than everyone else. Being confident is knowing who you are, good or bad, and what you have, great or small. Filled with flaws but love and accept all of you anyway, and never settle for the flaw and the bad, knowing the possibilities to improve are endless.

71. LOVE is a MUST. Relationship is a choice. When you choose your friends, you choose your destiny. Choose builder friends, not breaker friends. Choose a help mate, not a hindering spouse.

72. Beauty from the outside is a plus. Beauty from within is a must.

73. Behind some beautiful/lovely features are some deadly ugly creatures.

74. The good you do will always be remembered, even if it's not appreciated immediately.

75. Some things and people are just there to challenge your character, integrity, strength, and

intelligence. Be sure they are displayed with skills, class, confidence, and excellence.

76. If you keep giving everyone a piece of your mind, you will be left mindless. Instead, share your thoughts, and express your feelings.

77. The "Holy Hell" people are so holy that everyone else is going to hell except them. They have never sinned, so they cannot give anyone else a chance to grow in God. Nobody deserves a second chance. They don't believe God's word said, "Come as you are," or, "Though your sin is as scarlet, they shall be as wool." They send everyone to hell, even before God judges them. They are the Holy Hell folks.

78. When you are controlled by carnality, you see only in the natural, think in the flesh, are attracted by the flesh, and are seduced by the flesh. There is no room for spiritual things to flourish.

79. You cannot control what you conceal.

80. Arrogance sits on a high fence and parades itself by looking down on others with criticism. Arrogance is condescending in statements and comments. Arrogance humiliates with jokes.

81. Do not live a lie, pretending you are living in peace.

82. I am irreplaceable; there is only one me.

83. Reputation is worth more than a paycheck. And integrity is worth more than a career or popularity.

84. Having a spirit of excellence is excellent.

85. Self-improvement messages are different from salvation messages. One is psychological, and the other is spiritual.

86. Accept the changes in your life as they come. Some changes are inevitable, while others are optional. Don't keep going to the size six rack when you know it no longer fits you. You will be uncomfortable in that outfit. Leave that rack and go to what suits your present position or situation.

87. God is not recognized; He is revealed. Without revelation, we cannot recognize His power or presence.

88. A parasitic friend is one who takes from you, leans on you, and leeches on you with nothing to give in return, but drama and other people's stories.

89. It's okay to not be at your best every day. But it is not okay to stay at your worst all your life.

90. The right thing is not always legal, and the legal thing is not always right. There are times when decency and moral values are what's needed to fix things.

91. All the secrets that someone keeps holding over you, imagine what would happen if you took it from them by being honest about that thing? They will be holding their heads in shame instead.

92. I used to believe that "I am too blessed to be stressed" and felt guilty when I got overwhelmed until I found out it was a cliché. Even the best of us has our down days and disappointing moments that drain us.

93. There is no greater induction than when you are inducted by the God who created you.

94. God does not make a promise that he does not have the power to see come to pass.

95. Suppose you are waiting on God outside of God, you only hope He will. But if you are waiting on Him in Him, you know that He will deliver as promised.

96. Life happens. The facade of "putting on" for other people will eat you away. Do not allow yourself to get caught in the rift.

97. You cannot be a representation of construction and destruction at the same time. This only happens when you are tearing down the old and building the new.

98. In today's world, we find more folks discussing and craving authority than responsibility.

99. Authority, responsibility, and accountability go together.

100. When we realize that we must make repentance a lifestyle, even when we think that we have not sinned, we adopt an attitude of repentance. We are not only seeking God's forgiveness, but also, we gain humility and conscience.

101. The old man is carnality, fleshy/worldly desires, and actions. The old man is selfish and does not consider righteousness. He sins without remorse because the old man knows only sin. Until the new birth has happened, the old man will always win.

102. Real spiritual warfare is not the war you rage against others. It's when you war against yourself, the moment you start to wage war against the stuff you have on the inside that no one knows about.

103. Indecision is still a decision.

104. Learn the characteristics of eagles, both male and female. The female eagle tests her mate before she trusts him. The male eagle cannot mate with her if he does not pass the test. Eagles are totally committed to their mate, both male and female.

Bald Eagles are said to stay with their mates for life and only choose another mate if one dies.

105. You cannot allow someone who does not have power over you to defeat you.

106. It's time to stop your "BS" (Belief System) from blocking you from everything that could be yours. Your "BS" can be your blocker or opener.

107. Why live a lie to pretend you are living in peace?

108. You cannot bully or intimidate those who have the same passion or spirit as you.

109. Aggressiveness is what you use in competing. It should not be who you are.

110. Dirt is everywhere and easy to find. We all have some sort of dirt on us. So, when you try to find dirt on others, it will be easy to find. But the same is true if someone looks for dirt on you.

111. You are better than your predicament, which serves as a testament to your willpower.

112. Marketplaces do not use security because their products are cheap. Rolex, Tiffany & Co., Buccellati, etc., have security because they have value to secure. Which of them can you be identified with?

113. Personal revelation differs from collective revelation. Do not impose your revelation and conviction from God on others.

114. People may be plotting and planning what to do to you, but God Almighty is planning what to do for you.

115. God breaks every rule to accomplish His will. He is not subjected to rules or systems.

116. Confirmation from God is better than validation from man.

117. Ladies, use your charm to impact men, not to attract them.

118. Christians or not, we do not need to be or show sexy to the world. Sexy is for our husbands. What you ought to be, is, impacting and attracting.

119. Impacting lives positively and attracting people so they can be led to Christ.

120. Don't get too comfortable where you are. Always strive to get better, be better, and do better.

121. If a person cannot contribute to your happiness, you do not need them around you permanently. They will only infringe on what you already have.

122. Not everyone with you is "with" you.

123. Opposition is a sign that you are in position.

124. Those in authority do not allow small thinkers and talkers to influence them in decision-making and strategy.

125. Even if you lose, it does not mean you've failed. Don't complain.

126. Do not look up to the rich to worship him, nor down at the poor to scorn him. But see every man as a possibility: a possibility to gain and a possibility to lose.

127. The world is big enough for everyone. Take enough of what you need and leave the rest for others.

128. When the old is screaming at you, the new is whispering in your heart, "Transform."

129. Marriage is for the purpose of coming together as one—building, achieving, discovering, and experiencing good and bad, highs and lows, ups and downs—it is not a fair-weather agreement.

130. God will anoint you outside of the system, away from systematic eyes. Then let you walk into the system to challenge and change.

131. People will judge what's on you because they don't know what's in you.

132. "Going there" cannot tell "been there" how to get there.

133. Making an agreement is having the commitment before any type of commencement.

134. Failing is more profitable than quitting.

135. If your faith is not in line with the will of God, it's an ineffective faith.

136. No amount of clothes, makeup, perfume, cologne, hairstyle, or any superficial things can hide an ugly heart. If your heart is ugly and bitter, it will show after a while. Even if you say good things, and act well. Your heart will be detected. On the other hand, a person with a good heart will be seen and known even when they try to be mean.

137. Satan plans to sabotage the Servants of God and uses anything to do that. He will stop at nothing because he is determined to hold you down and keep you down. Whatever Satan can get his hands on to accomplish his evil plan, that is what he will use. Your finances, your health, your ministry, your friends, and your family. Anything and anyone.

138. Be prepared for the answer when you ask God to do something. Make sure you are ready spiritually, mentally, and emotionally to deal with God's response, and the result of His response to your request.

139. When God speaks, it does not need to go anywhere else for approval. God's word is forever settled, both on earth and in heaven.

They talk if you
are doing **GOOD**,
they talk if you are
doing **BAD**.

They talk just
because... Your
job is to remain
**COOL-CALM-
COLLECTIVE**
while you **FOCUS**.

@GeorgiaPeterkin

140. If you ever think or believe that as a child of God, you will never have problems, or go through hardship, that you will never be betrayed, lied against, lied to, owe bills, go through sickness, then you are WRONG. You are susceptible to issues and mishaps as long as you are on Earth. What we will have that will separate us from the unsaved is divine peace and assurance of hope because we are given the COMFORTER (Holy Spirit).

141. Sometimes, what we did not intend, becomes the effect that spoils everything.

142. When your brain and your heart are in sync, decisions are decisive. Thoughts and feelings collaborate to bring resolution to inner and outer conflicts. By extension, your common sense gets a chance to be showcased. Why? You may ask... That's because certain situations or things are not complicated as the heart or brain would want you to believe. All it takes is Common Sense (Practical Judgment).

143. When you pray to God, be sure you listen as well. Listening is twice as important as talking. Prayer is a dialogue between man and God. So, if you pour out your request to Him, be willing and able to wait for His response. Sometimes, you will have to linger there before He speaks.

144. What you can afford presently is not an indication of your worth.

145. If I'm the smartest in my circle, then I can't expect to be challenged. I need to be surrounded by others who will make me want to level up.

146. Suppose we are always afraid of losing to the point where we are chronically protective and playing it safe; how will we ever get a chance to win?

147. It is better to walk out with dignity than to be led out in shame.

148. There are times in our life when we must act for the greater good of those that depend on us, while knowing that we will not benefit from our selfless act.

149. Our greatest enemy, at times, is the one we look at in the mirror every day. And other times, it is the one we cannot see or touch, but we can feel (Love & Emotions).

150. Compromise is sometimes the only way forward to save what is worth saving.

151. Our difficulties and unfair experiences do not define us. We are defined by how we respond to them.

152. The simple find it difficult to understand the intelligent. But the intelligent can comprehend the simple. Therefore, the greater responsibility rests on the intelligence of the intelligent. Suppose we will affect change of any kind and impact people of all spheres. In that case, we must speak a language that is understood by all, including the simplest of minds. How we transfer information and communicate knowledge, inspiration, and education must be diversified.

153. Your ego, sometimes, allows you to admit and confess when you are wrong just to showcase arrogance.

154. Sometimes, you must throw out what you "think" you know and follow your instincts.

155. Maybe you are unprepared, but that does not disqualify you from the position meant for you.

156. It's human to err in judgment of character. It's also human to make an idiot of yourself by choosing to trust people by how they speak and present themselves. But it is disgusting and devilish to be a pathological misleader by your words and action.

157. Loyalty is the consequence of winning one's heart and trust. Trust is the consequence of actions that support your words consistently.

158. Being confronted with the truth, and denying it, is like saying Rome isn't on fire even while the thick smoke is going up.

159. Losing one fight in a whole battle can, sometimes, be the best strategy for winning the war.

160. You can lead me with a thread when you are sincere and honest, but a thousand cranes can't move me using deceit and trickery.

161. Sometimes, men can be tricky; what may look like 'want' may only want you for a short time until the one he really wants, wants him. You are just something to do until she comes to him.

162. When the permanent comes, the temporary is no longer necessary or needed.

163. Live on purpose and be intentional. Walk it out, live it out, act it out, work it out intentionally.

164. There is nothing wrong with "putting your best foot forward," but there's something wrong with you putting on a whole facade. That's just plain fake, false, and deceptive.

165. Right where you are, this moment, it's a good place to pause and just say, "LORD, I thank you." "LORD, I need you," "LORD, I bless you," "LORD, I praise you."

166. I am 100% perfectly imperfect. But I accept the totality of myself, all my imperfections. I make mistakes, and I've failed. I've won, and I've lost. I've been hurt, and I have hurt others. I cry, and I laugh. I feel sadness, I feel happiness, and I have felt pain. I have felt rejection, and I have rejected others, I have felt loved, and I have loved. I feel anger, I have blemishes, I get pimples, I walk around the house in T. Shirt, I eat in bed, I get gas, I've had bad hair days... I AM HUMAN.

167. Plans don't always turn out to be reality. But every successful reality is a result of a well-thought-thought-through plan.

168. Sometimes, you must blame yourself because you knew better.

169. I don't know how to sell a dream, but I can certainly work with a dream.

170. Lord, I thank you for salvation; I thank you for saving me from self-destruction.

171. A toxic relationship is not just limited to romantic couples. It's also parent-child/ren, sibling-sibling, other family members, co-workers, and friends.

172. A man without a vision for his future always returns to his past.

173. When you ask for the truth, it might come from an unfiltered mouth. Accept it anyway, and respect the person for being truthful, even if it's a brutal truth.

174. A real man, a respectable man, a mature man, does not need a woman to "build him" but a woman to build with him and beside him.

175. Don't ask anyone for anything, good or bad. Just observe the actions of people and accept or reject them accordingly.

176. There is no such thing as totally independent, totally intelligent, or totally wise. There is no totality or complete self-sufficiency or self-sustaining with human being.

177. Sometimes, people are scared to let go because they cannot see themselves anywhere or with anyone else. So, they stay in an abusive, unfaithful, and disloyal relationship, not knowing a bigger, brighter future awaits them.

178. We all have limitations as human beings; we're all ignorant of something. It's foolish to believe or act like we have the answer to or for everything. Or that we are always right. That is sheer pride and arrogance. Life will teach you otherwise.

179. A part of being strong is being humble.

180. Follow those who can and will lead you in Godly directions, not "Bird Box" blindfolded people bumping into everything, everyone, everywhere.

181. I respect people who say what they mean and mean what they say. Even if they are trashing your personality or calling you out on your crap.

182. We like to think that we do things for logical reasons. But in practice, our emotion supersedes our intellect in actions, words, and judgment.

183. Get to fully know yourself. Apart from what you have been taught, what you hear, what people think or say about you, how they feel about you and how they view you, get to know and understand YOU. Self-discovery is a marvelous thing; because through that, purpose and reasons are discovered. And when you have discovered your reason and purpose, your being here serves. Then there is no need for "resolutions" but always a passion for attainable goal setting. Everything is inside of you. You only need to discover YOU and develop, function, live and apply your God-given ability.

184. Sometimes, people speak out against certain actions, calling them unethical or tacky. But it is to ensure that it is not used as an option to expose their dirty deeds/character.

185. Sometimes, the person that annoys you the most is the one you really need. The annoyance is the provocation of growth, strength, love, accountability, capability, and independence — the things you don't want to work on.

186. The joy you feel when someone else succeeds will determine how you will be supported when you succeed. It is a ripple effect.

187. Every scar tells a story. Go and tell your story; let your scar speak. Don't hide your scar. Someone is waiting to read the story so they can get the courage to publish their scar, which will change or save a life.

188. The size of the scar does not represent the magnitude of the story. Small scars can tell big stories. The scar is small, but the wound is deep.

189. My power and position are not used to make me important. It is used to empower others.

190. Even professionals are prone to mistakes, hurt, deception, and rejection. The difference is that some may know how to handle and process what they are experiencing and how it makes them feel.

191. What I like most about myself is my "heart," and the thing I hate most about myself is my "heart." (The love, sincerity, purity, and compassion of it)

192. Sometimes, you play and play, thinking you are winning, and then you get outplayed by who you least expect. Moral: Don't be too comfortable in the games you play. The whistle has not yet blown.

193. Always leave enough room for disappointment and the unexpected because they WILL show up. But never let hope and positivity go; let them stay with you.

194. I am not a bitter woman; I am a better lady. All men are not the same; I do say there are some wonderful gentlemen out there still.

195. FOOLS do foolish things proudly and think they are wise. A fool will laugh at you while the joke is on them.

196. If you follow your feelings, you will fall into many regrettable situations. But following your "gut feelings" will avoid many regrettable situations.

197. Guilt, in its right place and context, is authorized and acceptable. Shame and shaming aren't.

198. Don't get so caught up in loving yourself and doing yourself well that you forget to love others and do well to others.

199. What is out of my control belongs to God. He handles all the difficult stuff. I don't play the hero.

200. Whether you are book-smart or street-smart, it does not matter how you hustle if it's honest work. Hard work is hard work and deserves to be recognized and rewarded.

201. Sometimes, less is more. Lesser friends, more peace. Fewer distractions, more focus. Less negativity, more positive energy, and outcome.

202. Indeed, a closed mouth will not get fed. But at the same time, a still tongue keeps a wise head. "Even a fool is considered wise when he keeps silent."

203. I am spiritually strong. I don't change for the world; the world changes to accommodate me.

204. I have survived too many storms to be threatened or concerned by a raindrop.

205. I am no longer spending my time. I am investing my time. Be it on people or things.

206. "People lie, but the pupil doesn't lie."

207. It's not so much the "intensity" but rather the "CONSISTENCY."

208. The great default and social ill of our world today are that we all blame someone else for our failures, mistakes, and unpleasant encounters. We only take credit for the good and praiseworthy events.

209. A serial abuser can train you to blame yourself and take false responsibility. Sarcasm and "gaslighting" are some of their tools.

" Someone of us are
EMOTIONALLY
FORTIFIED,
while others are
EMOTIONALLY
PETRIFIED.

@GeorgiaPeterkin

210. You may have made a mistake in the past, and that is fine. But it is not a license to remain silent for the rest of your life. Your voice, opinion, advice, and input still matter.

211. Strength is not in how you overcome or control a person. Strength is how you overcome and control yourself.

212. Timing and occasion are two critical tools when exploring or exploiting an opportunity.

213. If I lose friends or opportunities because of my honesty, then I never had either in the first place.

214. If logic and reasoning were subjects in school, many would have at least a bit of either or both. Unfortunately, that's not the case.

215. People may not appreciate you every day, even those you expect. But when someone shows appreciation and values you, it reignites your passion and drives you to be more and do more.

216. Life is all about seasons, and seasons change. Be flexible and go through each season by adapting to the changing times.

217. Revenge, sometimes, costs you something, but karma costs nothing. It pays to let karma do the work.

218. Refusing to hear the truth will not make the reality go away.

219. I may be servicing you from a lower position; that doesn't mean you are above me in standard or capacity.

220. Your connection might get you in the game, but your skills, value, and wisdom will keep you in it.

221. Be a magnet for beautiful things. Draw people to you through your sincere authenticity.

222. Go and be great; greatness is in you.

223. The new BBL is, "BOUNCE BACK, LADY." Strength is going to look good on YOU.

224. Not everyone you encounter you should connect with. Be like the ants; they exemplify the term; "keep it moving."

225. Before you think about giving up, relax, reset, refocus, reexamine, restart, rebuild, and reintroduce.

226. Two things that never lie. ENERGY and EYES. Learn to read them both.

227. I can do this, I will do this, I am doing this; I DID IT.

228. If you follow your feelings, you will fall into many regrettable situations. But if you follow your "Gut Feelings," you will avoid many regrettable situations.

229. Sometimes, people think they've found a fool. But in reality, they've been given a blessing that they are treating as a fool. Eventually, they lose the blessing and realize they are fools.

230. I know my worth. I have paid dearly for every ounce of it. So, excuse me if I'm GUARDED.

231. I have left, but I've not yet arrived. I am still on my journey to greatness and wisdom.

232. As a parent, there are many things you did or would do for your children, and many things you didn't and couldn't do because of your children.

233. There was a great flood that drowned a whole generation and sank boats, but that same flood; floated an ark with eight persons and a few animals. If God decides to keep you, nothing can destroy you. And if God decides to destroy you, nothing can keep you.

234. Invisibility can sometimes be an asset when working on your goals.

235. A dime has a circle, and so does a penny. But one has more value. The moral is-it's not the size of your circle that holds the value.

236. Jealousy and disrespect show up in compliments and jokes too. Be alert.

237. "Let us hear the conclusion of the whole matter: Fear God and keep His commandment. For this is the whole duty of man." Eccl 12:13

238. Some are emotionally fortified, while others are emotionally petrified.

239. They talk if you are doing well; they talk if you are not doing well. They talk just because... Your job is to remain cool, calm and collective while you focus.

240. Due to our flawed nature as human beings, we will inevitably cause harm and disappointments to others. Inadvertently or otherwise.

241. FAITH = Stability amid instability.

242. Everyone looks okay and is doing okay until you have a deep conversation with them.

243. Maybe you are not over him/her. But you are definitely over the toxic situation.

244. I don't say "I LOVE YOU" as a protocol or cliché. I say "I LOVE YOU" because I mean it.

245. Freedom Road feels liberating when it's what you've been longing for, even though you're unsure where you are going.

246. If you intentionally cause someone pain for a gain of any kind, you will eventually realize what you've gained is a total loss.

247. Growth and achievement in life requires different things at different times. Sometimes, you must isolate yourself like an eagle in molting, and at other times surround yourself with an alliance like a pack of lions.

248. Some things to remember:
    • Stepping back doesn't mean you are giving up.
    • Saying "NO" doesn't make you unkind.
    • Refusing to act or react is not a sign of fear.
    • Letting go does not indicate your weakness.
    • Taking care of yourself is not selfishness.

    The truth is, we need to learn the art of these things to maintain a balanced life. If not, we will be left totally dejected, depleted, and filled with should-haves and could-haves.

249. Why seek validation from those who are not valid? If you must, then let your validation come from those who have value, substance and credibility.

250. When sin becomes a life-long habit, it turns into hard-to-break stronghold that takes root and grows into a generational strongman in families.

251. Each day I am able to resist my negative and non-progressive urges is a WIN for me! I can look forward to the new challenge ahead with hope.

252. It takes immeasurable strength and bravery to survive every problem and challenge, and still retain your kindness, patience, love, courage and compassion.

253. Sometimes, when you get connected to people who claim to have pure intentions towards you, it takes wisdom, discerning ability and keen observation to detect their crafty ulterior motives because, as the serpent is subtle, so they are. These people can be found in your workplace, churches, random encounters, friends and family circle. Don't be hasty to let down your guard because of some assuasive speech.

254. Kindness and generosity never go out of style. However, they require wisdom and boundaries.

255. Takers have no limits; therefore, the responsibility falls solely on the givers to say NO MORE!

Here is something to ALWAYS have on your to-do list every day:

Get to know you. Know yourself fully—apart from what you have been taught by your parents, culture, systems, education, and environment, what you hear, what people think or say about you, how people feel about you, and how they view you. Get to know you and understand you.

Self-discovery is a marvelous thing. Through it, purpose and reasons are discovered. And when you discover the reason for being, and what the purpose of you being here serves, there will be no need for "resolutions," invalid validations and approvals. There will only be passion for/and dedication to attainable goal setting, purpose fulfilment, growth and self-acceptance. This, by no means, should allow you to live a selfish life, but one that will ignite you to leave a positive and impactful footprint behind.

Everything is inside you! You only need to discover you, and then develop, function, live and apply your God-given ability.

Remember! The only person who can dictate otherwise to you is your Creator, God Almighty, and He ALWAYS does have beautiful plans for YOU, once you have discovered YOU.

I leave you with this... Jeremiah 29:11

Shalom!

"

People recognize a
KIND HEART and
a **PURE** generous
soul. *But, be careful!*
There are those who
will get close to you
only to exploit your
KINDNESS and
GENEROSITY.

@GeorgiaPeterkin

WHAT I TELL MYSELF

_____

_____

_____

_____

_____

_____

_____

_____

_____

_____

_____

WHAT I TELL MYSELF

_____

_____

_____

_____

_____

_____

_____

_____

_____

_____

_____

WHAT I TELL MYSELF

_____

_____

_____

_____

_____

_____

_____

_____

_____

_____

_____

WHAT I TELL MYSELF

WHAT I TELL MYSELF

WHAT I TELL MYSELF

_____

_____

_____

_____

_____

_____

_____

_____

_____

_____

_____

WHAT I TELL MYSELF

_____

_____

_____

_____

_____

_____

_____

_____

_____

_____

_____

WHAT I TELL MYSELF

WHAT I TELL MYSELF

_____

_____

_____

_____

_____

_____

_____

_____

_____

_____

_____

_____

WHAT I TELL MYSELF

_____

_____

_____

_____

_____

_____

_____

_____

_____

_____

_____

_____

WHAT I TELL MYSELF

_____

_____

_____

_____

_____

_____

_____

_____

_____

_____

_____

WHAT I TELL MYSELF

_____

_____

_____

_____

_____

_____

_____

_____

_____

_____

_____

WHAT I TELL MYSELF

_____

_____

_____

_____

_____

_____

_____

_____

_____

_____

_____

WHAT I TELL MYSELF

_____

_____

_____

_____

_____

_____

_____

_____

_____

_____

_____

> Let us **HEAR** the conclusion of all the whole matter: **FEAR GOD** and keep **HIS COMMANDMENTS:** For this is the whole *duty of man*.

Ecle 12:13

@GeorgiaPeterkin

www.ingramcontent.com/pod-product-compliance
Lightning Source LLC
Chambersburg PA
CBHW060347130626
46553CB00003B/1127